SPOTLIGHT ON SOCIAL AND EMOTIONAL LEARNING

OVERCOMING OBSTACLES

IDENTIFYING PROBLEMS

RACHAEL MORLOCK

PowerKiDS press.

New York

Published in 2020 by The Rosen Publishing Group, Inc.
29 East 21st Street, New York, NY 10010

Editor: Elizabeth Krajnik
Designer: Michael Flynn

Photo Credits: Cover Jose Luis Pelaez Inc/DigitalVision/Getty Images; cover, pp. 1, 3–6, 8, 10–12, 14, 16–18, 20–24 (background) TairA/Shutterstock.com; p. 4 KDdesignphoto/Shutterstock.com; p. 5 Kathryn Scott/Denver Post/Getty Images; p. 7 Gorodenkoff/Shutterstock.com; p. 9 Keystone-France/Gamma-Keystone/Getty Images; p. 10 Jes2u.photo/Shutterstock.com; p. 11 Anna Nahabed/Shutterstock.com; p. 13 MIA Studio/Shutterstock.com; p. 15 JGI/Jamie Grill/Getty Images; p. 16 Stock Rocket/Shutterstock.com; p. 17 Studio Romantic/Shutterstock.com; p. 19 NASA/Hulton Archive/Getty Images; p. 20 Kdonmuang/Shutterstock.com; p. 21 Rido/Shutterstock.com; p. 22 Monkey Business Images/Shutterstock.com.

Cataloging-in-Publication Data

Names: Morlock, Rachael.
Title: Overcoming obstacles: identifying problems / Rachael Morlock.
Description: New York : PowerKids Press, 2020. | Series: Spotlight on social and emotional learning | Includes glossary and index.
Identifiers: ISBN 9781725306790 (pbk.) | ISBN 9781725306820 (library bound) | ISBN 9781725306806 (6pack)
Subjects: LCSH: Problem solving in children--Juvenile literature. | Interpersonal relations--Juvenile literature. | Decision making in children--Juvenile literature. | Social skills in children--Juvenile literature.
Classification: LCC BF723.P8 M675 2020 | DDC 153.4'3--dc23

Manufactured in the United States of America

CPSIA Compliance Information: Batch #CWPK20. For further information contact Rosen Publishing, New York, New York at 1-800-237-9932.

CONTENTS

WHAT'S THE PROBLEM? 4

HOW TO SOLVE PROBLEMS 6

IDENTIFYING PROBLEMS 8

KEEP CALM 10

FINDING THE WORDS 12

INVESTIGATE 14

TALK IT THROUGH 16

GETTING STUCK 18

DEVELOPING YOUR SKILLS 20

OVERCOMING OBSTACLES 22

GLOSSARY 23

INDEX 24

PRIMARY SOURCE LIST 24

WEBSITES 24

CHAPTER ONE

WHAT'S THE PROBLEM?

People use problem solving in many areas of their lives. Problem solving is a social skill that helps you build stronger **relationships** and friendships. It's an emotional skill that offers tools for working through your thoughts and feelings. It's a creative skill that can inspire you and help you come up with new ideas. It's a thinking skill that can help you overcome obstacles, or things in your way. It's a **physical** skill that can help you understand how things work together.

Gitanjali Rao was 11 years old when she created a quick and easy way to test water for lead, which is a poisonous heavy metal. Her problem-solving invention helps prevent people from drinking **contaminated** water.

It takes practice, but problem solving is a skill you already use every day for large and small problems. However, to solve a problem, you must first identify what the problem is. From there, you can follow steps to solve your problem. Exercising our problem-solving skills helps us lead happier and healthier lives.

CHAPTER TWO

HOW TO SOLVE PROBLEMS

How do you know if you have a problem? If there's a gap between what is and what should be, then there's a problem. Sometimes problems are personal. Then the gap lies between what you have and what you want. Once you recognize there's a problem, you can begin the problem-solving process.

The first step is identifying the problem. It may seem **obvious**, but understanding your problem is important for finding a **solution**. The second step is considering possible solutions. The third step is to **evaluate** your **options** and think about the possible consequences, or results, of each of your options. The fourth step is choosing a solution and trying it out. The fifth and final step is to reflect, or look back, on the results. If you didn't like the result of your solution, you may need to repeat steps four and five.

You can practice the problem-solving process with games, puzzles, and projects.

CHAPTER THREE

IDENTIFYING PROBLEMS

The first step of problem solving is often overlooked. If you're in a hurry to find a solution, you might want to jump ahead and begin trying different options. Unfortunately, this can lead to even more problems! Before you look for a solution, it's important to understand and identify your problem.

Take the time to get to the root of your problem. Otherwise, you might work on solving the wrong problem by focusing on a **symptom** instead of the true cause. This usually happens when people assume, or think they know but don't, that they understand a problem. Instead of assuming, take a scientific approach. Use observations and facts to identify the problem. This will help you clearly understand what needs to be done. As you work to identify the problem, there are a number of tips and methods that can help.

Scientist and mathematician Albert Einstein said, "If I were given one hour to save the planet, I would spend 59 minutes defining the problem and one minute resolving it."

CHAPTER FOUR

KEEP CALM

How do you feel when faced with a problem? Maybe you're having trouble learning a new swimming stroke or you keep forgetting to bring your lunch to school. Maybe you're having trouble understanding a math problem or you had a disagreement with a friend. A lot of problems are tied to your emotions. They can leave you feeling **frustrated**.

Meditation can be as simple as paying attention to your breathing. Close your eyes and slowly breathe in and out five times. Do you feel calmer and more focused?

It's easier to think clearly when you're calm. Try taking deep breaths or **meditating** to work through your frustration. Find a quiet place or just take some quiet time to yourself so you can listen to your thoughts. If you feel very upset, you might need to take a break before identifying your problem.

When you're calm and ready to identify your problem, focus on the facts. Try not to blame others. Instead, think about your own actions, which are the only things you can control.

CHAPTER FIVE

FINDING THE WORDS

In order to be calm, you may need to acknowledge, or recognize and accept, the feelings you're having. This is especially true if you have a social problem, like a disagreement with a friend or family member. Acknowledging your feelings takes self-awareness, or knowledge of your thoughts and emotions.

It can be hard to put your feelings into words. The more you know about emotions, the easier it will be to identify them. When you've acknowledged your feelings, you can try to understand what caused you to have them. Try to fill in the sentence, "I feel ____ when _____ happens."

Acknowledging your feelings brings you one step closer to identifying the problem. You've identified a problem when you can put it into words. You'll need to **describe** the problem as clearly as you can.

When you're identifying a problem, writing it down or saying it out loud can help.

CHAPTER SIX

INVESTIGATE

Your job now is to act like a problem-solving detective. It's time to investigate what's happening. Investigating means carefully looking into all parts of your situation to find and understand the problem.

Use the question words—who, what, where, when, why, and how—as a starting point for thinking about the problem. How do you know there's a problem? Who's involved in, or connected to, the problem? What's happening? When's it happening? Where's it happening? Why's it happening?

Let's say that you missed the bus again. Missing the bus is a problem, but investigating might help you realize that the problem is actually a symptom of a different problem—you don't have enough time to get ready in the morning. Identifying the problem correctly can lead you to the best solutions.

Getting all the facts about your situation will help you figure out the best solution for your problem. You may even find some things you overlooked!

CHAPTER SEVEN

TALK IT THROUGH

Problem solving is a skill that improves with time and practice. The parts of your brain that help you solve problems develop, or grow and get stronger, as you get older. As you learn to solve problems, it can help to talk with a trusted adult or older friend. Sometimes, just talking about a problem can help you see the facts more clearly.

Talking to someone else about your problem can help you see it from a new perspective, or point of view.

Even when you ask for help, it's important to do the work yourself. An adult can guide you by asking questions or making suggestions instead of telling you the best solution. In the end, you're more likely to solve a problem if you understand it in your own words and use your own creative ideas.

Your class, sports team, or family might have a problem as a group. In this case, you can work together to identify problems and find solutions.

CHAPTER EIGHT

GETTING STUCK

Problems can be **complex**, confusing, and hard to identify. Everyone gets stuck sometimes, but this doesn't mean you should give up. Use your creativity and try to look at the problem from new perspectives. Look closely at things you may have overlooked when you were investigating the problem.

When a Mars **probe** disappeared in 1999, NASA scientists realized something had gone wrong, but they didn't know what. To figure out what happened to the probe, they had to identify the problem. They found that the probe's creators and operators had used different measuring systems. As a result, the probe traveled too quickly toward Mars and was destroyed. To identify the problem, NASA looked carefully at what happened. The problem was so small and unexpected that it was hard to find. It's important to keep looking until you identify the problem.

This Mars probe disappeared and was destroyed because of a miscommunication between teams. NASA scientists and engineers were able to identify the problem and avoid making the same mistake again.

CHAPTER NINE

DEVELOPING YOUR SKILLS

Every problem is different. You might need to try new and creative strategies, or methods, to identify it correctly. As you practice, you will find your own tricks for thinking clearly, investigating, and getting to the bottom of a problem.

Problem-solving skills don't develop on their own. They require hard work. However, each time you practice you strengthen your skills.

No matter what problem you face, working through it will help you with problems in the years to come. Problem-solving skills are like muscles. The more you use them, the stronger and more developed they become. As you learn to identify problems, you can use that problem-solving skill in many different areas. Thinking about a math problem might seem different than finding a way to include all your friends in a game, but you can use the same skills and steps to solve each problem. Solving and identifying everyday problems prepares you to work on larger, more complex problems.

CHAPTER TEN

OVERCOMING OBSTACLES

Identifying a problem is the first step to overcoming any obstacle. It can help if you stay calm, acknowledge and name your emotions, carefully investigate the issue, and talk or think through the problem. The more detailed you are in identifying your problem, the easier it will be to find the best solution. Once you can clearly identify the problem, you're ready to move on to the next problem-solving step.

Learning to solve problems is one of the best ways to work toward success. Whether you're focused on school, sports, or social challenges, you can use problem-solving skills to learn and grow. Developing these skills makes you more independent in facing challenges on your own. It can build up your confidence, or the feeling or belief that you can do something well or succeed at something. Keep practicing, and problem solving can help you reach your goals.

GLOSSARY

complex (kahm-PLEKS) Having to do with something with many parts.

contaminated (kuhn-TAA-muh-nay-tuhd) Polluted.

describe (dih-SKRIYB) To tell about in detail.

evaluate (ih-VAHL-yuh-wayt) To judge the importance, worth, or quality of something.

frustrated (fruh-STRAY-tuhd) Feeling angered or let down.

meditate (MEH-duh-tayt) To spend time in quiet thought.

obvious (AHB-vee-uhs) Easy to see or notice.

option (AHP-shuhn) Something that can be chosen.

physical (FIH-zih-kuhl) Existing in a form you can touch or see.

probe (PROHB) An unmanned craft used to send information about a body in space back to scientists on Earth.

relationship (rih-LAY-shuhn-ship) A connection with someone else.

solution (suh-LOO-shuhn) Something that solves a problem.

symptom (SIHMP-tuhm) A sign of something.

INDEX

C
confidence, 22
consequences, 6

E
Einstein, Albert, 8
emotions, 10, 12, 22

F
facts, 8, 11, 14, 16
feelings, 4, 12, 22
frustration, 11

I
ideas, 4, 17

M
meditation, 11

N
NASA, 18

O
observations, 8
options, 6, 8

P
perspective, 16, 18
practice, 5, 16
problem solving, 4, 5, 8, 16, 22

R
Rao, Gitanjali, 5
relationships, 4

S
self-awareness, 12
skill, 4, 5, 16, 20, 21, 22
solution, 6, 8, 14, 17, 22
steps, 5, 6, 22
strategies, 20
symptom, 8, 14

T
thoughts, 4, 12

W
words, 12, 14, 17

PRIMARY SOURCE LIST

Page 5
Gitanjali Rao, 11. Photograph. Kathryn Scott. November 7, 2017. *Denver Post* via Getty Images.

Page 9
Albert Einstein writing a mathematical formula on a blackboard. Photograph. Keystone-France. January 1, 1930. Gamma-Keystone via Getty Images.

Page 19
Mars Orbiter Probe. Rendering. NASA. September 1, 1999. Hulton Archive via Getty Images.

WEBSITES

Due to the changing nature of Internet links, PowerKids Press has developed an online list of websites related to the subject of this book. This site is updated regularly. Please use this link to access the list: www.powerkidslinks.com/SSEL/identifying